FIFE COUNCIL LIBRARIES

FC789278

KT-399-987

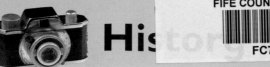

Homes

Sarah Ridley

FRANKLIN WATTS
LONDON • SYDNEY

SCHOOLS LIBRARY SERVICE

First published in 2007 by Franklin Watts

Copyright © Franklin Watts 2007

Franklin Watts
338 Euston Road
London NW1 3BH

Franklin Watts Australia
Level 17/207 Kent Street
Sydney, NSW 2000

All rights reserved.

Series editor: Sarah Peutrill
Art director: Jonathan Hair
Design: Jane Hawkins

A CIP catalogue record for this book is available from
the British Library.

Dewey number: 728
ISBN: 978 0 7496 7068 9

Printed in China

Franklin Watts is a division of Hachette Children's Books.

Picture credits:
Advertising Archives: 23b.
Beamish Museum: 12t, 18, 24, 26.
Colchester Museum Service: endpapers and 19t.
Edifice: 6t, 6b, 7t, 7b, 8b, 9, 10t
Mary Evans Picture Library: 8t, 16,
Getty Images: front cover main, 13, 15, 17t, 17b, 23t
Hulton Archive/Getty Images: 25b.
Leeds Library and Information Service: 10b, 11t, 11b
Andrea Leone/Shutterstock: front cover top.
Chris Makepeace: 20.
Museum of Rural Life, Reading: 3, 14,
National Monuments Record: 27t.
NMPFT Daily Herald Archive/Science & Society Picture
Library: 21.
Popperfoto: 12b
Science & Society Picture Library: 19c, 22, 25.
Courtesy of Rachel Tonkin and family: 27b.
Victoria & Albert Museum Images: 28.
Every attempt has been made to clear copyright. Should
there be any inadvertent omission please apply to the
publisher for rectification.

FIFE COUNCIL SCHOOLS	
789278	
PETERS	14-Aug-07
J728	£11.99
JPAS	AD

Home Sweet Home

Home! Sweet, sweet home!
There's no place like home.
There's no place like home.

Popular Victorian song, 1822
by J H Payne

Contents

SCHOOLS LIBRARY SERVICE

New homes

Where do you call home? People live in all kinds of homes – flats, houses, bungalows, caravans and even boats. Many homes were built in the last 20 years, like the ones on this page.

These houses are on a housing estate in a town. Look at the front doors to find two smaller houses and one bigger one with a garage.

This new house stands on its own in the countryside. It has been built in an old style.

Flats are stacked up on top of each other, so they use less space on the ground.

These houses are built from wood, recycled bricks and steel. Fewer new materials were used to build them than most houses. The roofs collect rainwater for use inside the homes.

Old homes

Many people live in houses built a long time ago. Lots of different families have lived in these houses. Older houses have often been repaired and changed by their many owners.

Built: between 1100 and 1200

This is one of the oldest houses in England. It is built of stone, a material that can last a long time. It is now a shop but it was the home of a wealthy family.

Built: between 1300 and 1400

This house was built for wealthy people 600 years ago. It has a timber frame, filled in with wattle and daub (wood, straw and mud).

Built: 1786

The windows and door are evenly spaced across the front of this house. Houses built at this time were made from brick, with wooden doors and window frames.

Be a history detective

- Look at the oldest house to find carved arches above windows and doors. Where else have you seen doorways and windows like these?

- Look at the house built between 1300 and 1400 to see a thatched roof. Thatch is made of reeds or straw.

- Which house would you like to live in?

Victorian homes

Millions of families today live in homes built when Queen Victoria was on the throne (1837–1901). At this time, a huge number of people moved from the countryside to towns and cities. Many houses of all sizes were built for them to live in.

Terraced houses join one to the other all along the street. Each of these houses was built with about six rooms.

Built: 1880s

Date: 1889

A wealthy Victorian family sit on the steps of their large home. Their home had twice as many rooms as the houses in the photo above.

While their workers usually lived in tiny houses, factory owners built huge houses for themselves, like this house, Gledlow Hall in Leeds.

Date: 1900

Date: 1901

Often, more than one family lived in these small, damp homes for Victorian factory workers. Over time, these homes have been knocked down and replaced.

Be a history detective

- Victorian houses often have a date on the front that tells you when they were built. See if you can find any in your area.
- What were Victorian houses built from?

Room to relax

Most homes have a room where you can sit down and relax. By the 1940s and 1950s, many families relaxed in the living room by listening to the radio, or watching the television.

Date: c. 1890

An old couple and their grandchild relax in their kitchen/living room. Many small homes only had one room downstairs.

A wealthy Victorian family listen to a woman playing the piano in the drawing room. Large Victorian homes had several living rooms.

Date: 1895

By the late 1950s, many homes had a television in the living room. Since then, people have often arranged their living room around the television.

Date: 1958

Be a history detective

- How does your family relax at home? Do you do any of the things in the photos?
- Does the TV look like yours?
- Ask your parents and grandparents how they relaxed at home when they were children.

Decorating styles

The way we decorate our homes has always changed with fashion. Wealthy Victorians filled their rooms with furniture, paintings and ornaments. Since then, people have gradually had fewer things in their homes.

Victorian ladies read their books in a room filled with furniture and objects. The Victorians loved deep colours and patterned wallpapers, fabrics and carpets.

Date: 1892

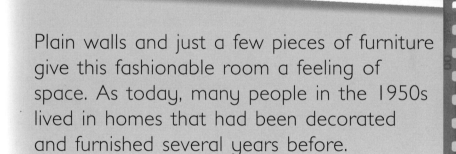

Date: 1955

Plain walls and just a few pieces of furniture give this fashionable room a feeling of space. As today, many people in the 1950s lived in homes that had been decorated and furnished several years before.

Be a history detective
- How many different patterns can you find in the oldest photograph?
- Compare the two rooms. Which things are the same and which are different?
- Which room do you like?

The kitchen

Around 100 years ago, the coal-fired range was the centre of the kitchen. Any washing-up or vegetable cleaning happened in the scullery close by. Over time, people have fitted kitchens with a sink, a cooker, a fridge, maybe a dishwasher, or even a dining table if there is room.

Date: 1860

A Victorian maid kneels to light the coal fire in the range that was used for cooking and heating water. Wealthy families could afford to pay a maid to cook and clean for them.

Date: 1950

A housewife prepares a meal in her bright new kitchen. Her kitchen has a gas cooker, cupboards, a sink with hot and cold taps and a work surface.

Date: 1975

This fashionable 1970s kitchen is lined with cupboards and has an electric hob.

Be a history detective

- Can you find the candles in the oldest photo? Do you know why they are there?
- What objects can you see in the pictures that you have in your kitchen?

Doing the washing

Most homes today have a washing machine, but 100 years ago people did their washing by hand in the scullery, washhouse or outside. During the 1940s and 1950s, more families could afford a washing machine at home.

Sisters do the weekly washing. The one on the left is using a dolly stick to swish the dirty clothes around in hot water. Her sister is wringing the clean clothes to squeeze out the water.

Date: c. 1910

It is washday and all down the row clothes hang out to dry.

Date: 1931

Date: c. 1948

This housewife is delighted with her new washing machine. She is using the mangle (on the top of the machine) to squeeze out the water.

Be a history detective

- Look for a washboard leaning up against the dolly tub in the oldest photo. Women scrubbed really dirty clothes against a washboard, using a block of soap, before washing them in the dolly tub.

- How is your washing machine different from the c. 1948 machine?

Housework

Until the 1960s, many women spent hours every day sweeping, brushing, mopping, scrubbing and dusting. Gradually machines, such as the vacuum cleaner, have made housework easier.

Date: c. 1910

A woman and a young boy scrub doorsteps to make them white again. Look for the metal bucket that the boy is using.

Date: 1930s

A woman vacuums the sofa. Before vacuum cleaners were invented, women had to brush furniture, carpets and rugs, or take them outside and beat them to get rid of the dust.

Be a history detective

- Does the vacuum cleaner look like the one in your home?
- Ask your grandparents whether they helped clean the house when they were children. Did they use the same equipment as we do today?

21

Keeping clean

Homes have not always had bathrooms. People washed in the bedroom, using soap and a bowl of water. About 120 years ago, builders started to include bathrooms in new houses, or to add them to older ones. However, some poorer families lived without bathrooms until about 50 years ago.

Date: c. 1900

It is time for the weekly bath on a sunny day. The tin bath has been filled with buckets of hot water from the range (see page 16). Usually the family bathed inside, in front of the fire, and everyone used the same water.

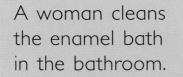

Date: 1951

A woman cleans the enamel bath in the bathroom.

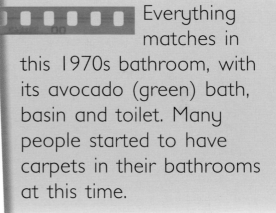

Everything matches in this 1970s bathroom, with its avocado (green) bath, basin and toilet. Many people started to have carpets in their bathrooms at this time.

Date: 1970s

Be a history detective

- Ask your grandparents what their bathroom was like? Did it have a shower?

- What is your bath made of? Find out what baths were made of in the past.

Bedrooms

Bedrooms used to be for sleeping and for getting washed and dressed. Since the 1950s and 1960s, they have also become places to play in, do homework, listen to music and entertain friends.

Date: 1900

A simple brass bed stands in this Victorian bedroom. As the toilet was usually outside, people kept a chamber pot under the bed to use during the night.

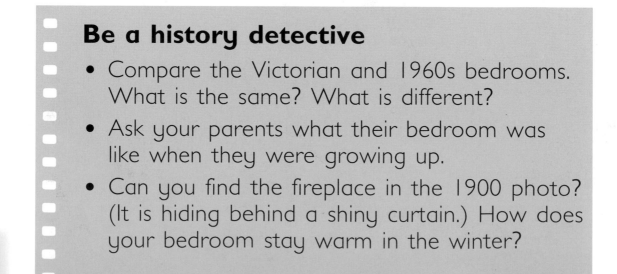

Be a history detective

- Compare the Victorian and 1960s bedrooms. What is the same? What is different?

- Ask your parents what their bedroom was like when they were growing up.

- Can you find the fireplace in the 1900 photo? (It is hiding behind a shiny curtain.) How does your bedroom stay warm in the winter?

A family crowd into the bedroom/living room of their home. These people could only afford to rent one room, with a tiny kitchen attached.

Date: 1934

Children play in their bedroom, a fun place to be.

Date: 1965

Gardens and yards

In the past, as today, people enjoyed creating gardens for their homes. They wanted an outdoor space for the family to relax in and somewhere to grow pretty flowers, as well as fruit and vegetables.

Date: 1913

The maid waits while the family enjoy tea in the garden. Wealthy families employed gardeners to look after lawns, orchards, flowerbeds and kitchen gardens.

Date: 1946

Children play with toys in the yard behind their homes. Many small homes had no gardens, so children played in the yard or on streets nearby.

Sisters play on the swings at the end of the garden. By the 1980s, many children had swings or a slide in their family's garden.

Date: 1980

Be a history detective

- What else is happening in the 1946 yard?
- Can you find a pushchair and a pram in the photos? Are they like modern ones?
- Look at the children's clothes. They give clues to when each photograph was taken.

The dolls' house, 1890

This dolls' house shows a Victorian home in tiny detail. Can you find the fireplace in every room? How is each room being used? Can you name the different rooms?

Glossary

c. (circa) This word means 'about' and is used with a date, like c. 1920, when it isn't known exactly when something happened.

Chamber pot A china pot with a handle that was used as a potty during the night.

Dolly tub/stick A wooden barrel (dolly tub) and long wooden pronged stick (dolly stick) used to wash clothes in the past.

Drawing room Another name for a living room, or sitting room.

Fabric A material such as cotton or wool.

Gradually Slowly over time.

Housing estate An area of housing where most of the houses were built within a short space of time.

Kitchen garden A walled vegetable garden.

Mangle A machine for squeezing water out of clothes. Someone turned the handle to pull wet clothes between two rollers.

Ornament Small objects, such as china animals, used to decorate the home.

Scullery A small room near the kitchen, used mainly during Victorian times, for doing the washing or preparing vegetables.

Terrace A row of houses that are joined to each other.

Victorian Relating to the years when Queen Victoria reigned (1837–1901). Victorian houses were built at that time.

Washhouse A room or small building made especially for washing clothes and sheets.

Wealthy Having a lot of money.

Index

Further information

Books

Ways Into History: Houses and Homes by Sally Hewitt (Franklin Watts)

A Victorian Childhood: At Home by Ruth Thomson (Franklin Watts)

Websites

www.wealddown.co.uk/poplar-cottage-construction-thatch-wattle-and-daub.htm
A website which shows how a timber-framed building is put together, including the thatched roof.

www.bbc.co.uk/education/dynamo/history/stepback.shtml
Learn about homes 100 years ago on this lively website.

www.woodlands-junior.kent.sch.uk/homework/houses.html
A really useful website about homes in the past, including Victorian homes.

Note to parents and teachers: Every effort has been made by the Publishers to ensure that these websites are suitable for children, that they are of the highest educational value, and that they contain no inappropriate or offensive material. However, because of the nature of the Internet, it is impossible to guarantee that the contents of these sites will not be altered. We strongly advise that Internet access is supervised by a responsible adult.